the print room

THE DEAD DOGS
BY JON FOSSE

Translated from the Norwegian
by May-Brit Akerholt

The Dead Dogs received its UK premiere
on 15 March 2014 at The Print Room, London.

The Dead Dogs received its world premiere
at Rogaland Theatre on 30 April 2004.

The Dead Dogs
by Jon Fosse
Translated from the Norwegian by May-Brit Akerholt

The Mother	Valerie Gogan
The Young Man	Danny Horn
The Friend	William Troughton
The Brother-in-law	Sam Redford
The Sister	Jennie Gruner

Director	Simon Usher
Set and Costume Designer	Libby Watson
Lighting Designer	Simon Bennison
Sound Designer	Paul Bull

Production Manager	Andy Beardmore
Stage Manager	Emma Tooze
Set Builders	Scenic Productions Ltd
Scenic Painter	Tash Shepherd
Costume Assistant	Amity MacDonnell
Wardrobe Supervisor	Grace Quin

Special Thanks to:
Paolo and Aud Cuniberti, Luke Holbrook,
Mel Kenyon, William Lavelle, The Norwegian Embassy, Anne Ulset,
Toby Whale

VALERIE GOGAN
The Mother

Valerie trained at LAMDA and has worked extensively in theatre, film and television.

Theatre credits include *The Secret Rapture, He Who Saw Everything* (National Theatre), *Worlds Apart* (Royal Shakespeare Company), *Love's Labour's Lost* (Manchester Royal Exchange), *A Doll's House* and *Abigail's Party* (Theatre Clwyd), *When is A Clock* (Grey Light Prods.), *A Day in the Death of Joe Egg, Pericles, The Winter's Tale* and *Clothe The Naked* (Leicester Haymarket), *Widowers' Houses* (Palace Theatre, Watford), *In Flame* (Bush Theatre), *Arden of Faversham* (Old Red Lion), *Warm* (Theatre503) and *Hamlet* (Rapture Theatre). In the West End she has appeared in *Les Liasons dangereuses* (Ambassadors Theatre) and *The Rehearsal* (Almeida/Garrick Theatre). She was in N.F. Simpson's final play, *If So, Then Yes* (Jermyn Street Theatre), and most recently in Catherine Johnson's *Shang-A-Lang* (King's Theatre, Glasgow).

Her films include *Dangerous Liasons, One More Kiss, As You Like It, The Jealous Sister, I Am Dead, Animal, Honey and Razorblades* and *Junkhearts*.

Leading roles on television include *Hamish MacBeth, Heart of the High Country, David Copperfield, Gawain and The Green Knight, Arriverderci Millwall, The Mrs Bradley Mysteries, Silent Witness*, Gertrude in the BBC's *Prefaces to Shakespeare* and most recently *50 Ways to Kill Your Lover*.

DANNY HORN
The Young Man

Danny trained at Central School of Speech and Drama.

His theatre credits include Junior in *The Revenger's Tragedy* (Hoxton Hall).

Film and television includes the lead role of Luke in feature film *Scar Tissue* (Sterling Pictures), *Legend of the Boogeyman* (UFO Films), *MI High* (CBBC) and a guest lead in *A Christmas Carol*, the 2010 Christmas special episode of *Doctor Who* (BBC) in which he played a young Michael Gambon.

Short films include *Perimeter Fence* (Shudder Films) and *Catalyst*.

WILLIAM TROUGHTON
The Friend

Theatre credits include: *The Ladykillers* (West End and UK Tour), *The Woman in Black* (West End), *Happy New* (Trafalgar Studios), *When Darkness Falls* (Beau Sejour).

TV: *Silk* (BBC) and *Crimson Field* (BBC).

Film: *Armistice*

SAM REDFORD
The Brother-in-law

Theatre credits include: *Hedda Gabler* (Hartford Stage), *The 39 Steps* (City Theatre, Pittsburgh), *The Belle of Belfast* (Cherry Lane Theatre, NYC), *Rock N Roll* (PICT, Pittsburgh), *The History Boys* (PICT, Pittsburgh), *The Seafarer* (City Theatre, Pittsburgh), *Mother Teresa is Dead* (City Theatre, Pittsburgh), *The Willis Girls* (Show of Strength), *Twelfth Night* (Southwark Playhouse).
Film: *The Warehouse, Deadtime Stories 2, The Slammin' Salmon, The Hurt Locker, Color me Kubrick, K-19 The Widowmaker.*
TV: *Casualty, One Life to Live, The Mayflower, Dirt War, Foyle's War, Doctors, Second Sight.*

JENNIE GRUNER
The Sister

Jennie Gruner studied at The Central School of Speech & Drama. Whilst training she was cast as 'Julia' in feature film *Zero* (Sterling Pictures, Dir. David Barrouk, Exec Prod. Nicolas Roeg), due to be released later this year.
Other credits include Petal in *Above & Beyond* (Corinthia Hotel, Look Left Look Right, 2013), *Dogs* (Tristan Bates Theatre, 2013), *Press Pass* (Bush Theatre, 2012), *London: Four Corners One Heart* (Theatre503, 2012), *Seduced* (Dir. Michael Kingsbury) and most recently appeared in *A Tale of Two Cities* (King's Head), *Terms & Conditions* (Stepping Out Theatre). She shot the role of Ellie in Television Comedy Pilot *This is Steve*, and the lead in LSFF short film winner *Come Clean*. Jennie has just shot the film *120 Days* and will next film *The Great Fire* (ITV).
She was voted one of the 'Rising Stars of 2013' by *The London Magazine*.

JON FOSSE
Playwright

Jon Fosse was born in Haugesund, Norway and currently divides his time between Olso, Austria and Bergen. Jon has written novels, short stories, poetry, children's books, essays and numerous plays. His work has been translated into more than thirty languages and his plays are performed all over the world. Jon Fosse has been the recipient of numerous awards including Hedda's Prize of Honour, the most prestigious award in Norwegian theatre and Austria's Nestroy Prize for Best Author. In 2005 Jon Fosse was made a Commander in the Royal Norwegian Order of St. Olav and in 2007 he was made a Knight in France's National Order of Merit. Jon Fosse was awarded the International Ibsen Award, 2010. In 2011, Fosse was granted the Grotten, an honorary residence located on the premises of the Royal Palace in Oslo; an honour which is specially bestowed by the King of Norway for contributions to Norwegian arts and culture.

Oberon Books publishes Plays One (*Someone Is Going to Come, The Name, The Guitar Man, The Child*), Plays Two (*A Summer's Day, Dream of Autumn and Winter*), Plays Three (*Mother and Child, Sleep my Baby Sleep, Afternoon, Beautiful, Death Variations*). Plays Four (*And We'll Never Be Parted, The Son, Visits, Meanwhile the Lights Go Down and Everything Becomes Black*), Plays Five (*Suzannah, Living Secretly, The Dead Dogs, A Red Butterfly's Wing, Warm, Telemakos, Sleep*). *Nightsongs, The Girl on the Sofa* and *I Am The Wind*. Plays Six (*Rambuku, Freedom, Over There, These Eyes, Girl in Yellow Raincoat, Christmas Tree Song and Sea*) will be published in May 2014.

MAY-BRIT AKERHOLT
English translation

May-Brit Akerholt is a freelance translator and dramaturg. More than 20 of her translations have been produced by leading theatre companies around Australia. She worked as production dramaturg for most of the productions. She has extensive experiences as production dramaturg on classic and contemporary plays. She has also worked as a dramaturg with a number of Australian playwrights in the development of their new plays. She is the Norwegian contemporary playwright Jon Fosse's English translator. Currently she is working with The Ibsen Centre at the University of Oslo on a new translation of a volume of Ibsen's letters and theatre articles.

Two volumes of May-Brit's translations of plays by Ibsen and Strindberg are published by Five Islands Press, University of Wollongong. Three volumes of her translations of Jon Fosse's plays are published by Oberon Books, London, with a fourth volume to appear in 2014. Her critical articles have been published in various books and journals, and her book, *Patrick White* (Australian Playwrights Monograph Series), was published by Rodopi, Amsterdam.

Positions include: Tutor in the School of English and Linguistics at Macquarie University; Lecturer in Drama at the National Institute of Dramatic Art (NIDA); six years as Resident Dramaturg at Sydney Theatre Company; ten years as Artistic Director of the Australian National Playwrights' Centre and the National Playwrights' Conference. She recently finished a PhD (*The Dramaturgy of Translation*) at the University of Sydney.

SIMON USHER
Director

Simon has directed widely in the UK. Recent productions include *The Complaint* (Hampstead Theatre), *Ivy & Joan* (The Print Room), *Splendid Isolation* (Edinburgh Festival), and *If So, Then Yes,* NF Simpson's final play (Jermyn Street). Other credits include *Tamar's Revenge, King Baby* (RSC), *The World's Biggest Diamond, Black Milk, Mother Teresa is Dead, Herons* (Royal Court), *Sing Yer Heart Out For The Lads* (National Theatre), *The Evil Doers, Pond Life, Not Fade Away, The Mortal Ash, All of You Mine, Looking At You (Revived) Again, Wishbones, Card Boys* (Bush Theatre), *Holes in the Skin, Mr Puntilla and His Man Matti* (Chichester Festival Theatre), *Great Balls of Fire* (Cambridge Theatre, West End), *No Man's Land* (English Touring Theatre) *Burning Everest, Exquisite Sister* (West Yorkshire Playhouse).

He has been Artistic Director of The Belgrade Theatre, Coventry (many productions, including *Hamlet* and *Waiting For Godot*), Associate Director of Leicester Haymarket (numerous productions, including *Timon of Athens, Pericles, The Winter's Tale* and *French Without Tears*) and Literary Manager of the Royal Court.

LIBBY WATSON
Set and Costume designer
Libby trained at Bristol Old Vic Theatre School and has a 1st class BA Hons in Theatre Design from Wimbledon School of Art.
Libby has worked extensively in the UK at the Royal Court, Birmingham Rep, The Crucible, The Wolsey, Nottingham Playhouse, Soho Theatre, Northcott Exeter, Bristol Old Vic, Bolton Octagon, Salisbury Playhouse, English Touring Theatre, Hampstead, West Yorkshire Playhouse, Riverside Studios, Hampstead Theatre, Tricycle, Stratford East, Bury St Edmunds Theatre Royal, Belgrade Coventry, Bush Theatre and Manahattan Theatre Club New York. Libby designed the 2011 Olivier Award winning play *The Mountaintop* at Trafalgar Studios West End. Recently she designed *One Monkey Don't Stop No Show* at the Tricycle, *God of Carnage* at Royal and Derngate Northampton and *Fences* by August Wilson at the Duchess Theatre West End. Future projects include *Propoganda Swing* at Nottingham Playhouse and the Belgrade Coventry and *As You Like It* at the Stafford and Ludlow 2014 Shakespeare Festival.

SIMON BENNISON
Lighting Designer
Simon trained in Music at Salford University, Lighting and Design at RADA and the Yale School of Drama, and in Architecture at the University of North London.
Works for theatre include: *Ivy & Joan* (The Print Room), *The Complaint, Everything is Illuminated* (Hampstead Theatre), *Splendid Isolation* (Edinburgh Festival), *Twelfth Night* (Ludlow Festival), *Comedians* (Hammersmith Lyric), *The Price* (Tricycle Theatre/West End), *The World's Biggest Diamond, Black Milk* (The Royal Court), *Home, Serjeant Musgrave's Dance, Comedians, The Contractor* and *Troilus & Cressida* (Oxford Stage Company/West End), *Yard, Normal,* and *Howie The Rookie* (Bush Theatre/Off Broadway), *Holes in the Skin* (Chichester Festival Theatre), *Scenes from an Execution, A Lie of the Mind* (Dundee Repertory Theatre), *Two Gentlemen of Verona* (Cottesloe), *The Lady's Not For Burning* (Finborough Theatre), *Death of a Faun* (Touring/Off Broadway), *Owner Occupier* (Arcola), and *Penthesilia, Anatol* (RADA). *Scenes from an Execution* was nominated for Best Lighting Design in the 2004 Critic's Awards for Theatre in Scotland.

PAUL BULL
Sound Designer

Paul provides sound and music – and other technical – support for all types of live performance. In addition, he is a sound artist, composes electronic music and performs as a musician using no-input mixing techniques.

Paul has a long history working with director Simon Usher, and productions include *Ivy & Joan* (The Print Room Balcony), *The Complaint* (Hampstead Downstairs), and *Terms and Conditions* (White Bear). Other recent sound designs include the Bike Shed Theatre's tour of *Bunnies (for short)*, *Sons Without Fathers*, *Uncle Vanya* and *Palace of the End* at the Arcola, and *Blok/Eko* for The Wrestling School at Exeter Northcott. Since 2000, Paul has been sound designer on many Edinburgh shows including Fringe First winners *Lockerbie:Unfinished Business*, *An Instinct for Kindness* and *Somewhere Beneath It All A Small Fire Burns, Still*. As a sound engineer, Paul enjoys working with Camille O'Sullivan, The Segue Sisters, Mike Westbrook, The Pindrop Band, piano*circus*, Exeter Contemporary Sounds, and Murray Lachlan Young. Away from theatre, Paul is a Labour and Co-op councillor on Exeter City Council and campaigns for social justice as a volunteer with Exeter Citizens Advice Bureau.

the print room

The Print Room is an intimate performing arts venue in Notting Hill that opened in 2010. Set just off Westbourne Grove, in a 1950's converted graphic design warehouse, it comprises an 80-seat flexible theatre and adjoining exhibition space. We have so far presented four highly acclaimed seasons of performing and visual arts across all genres including theatre, dance, concerts, exhibitions, and a varity of multidisciplinary collaborations.

Recent highlights include the London revivals of Harold Pinter's THE DUMB WAITER; Arthur Miller's THE LAST YANKEE and Brian Friel's MOLLY SWEENEY (which transferred to The Lyric Theatre, Belfast this year); the UK Premiere of Amy Herzog's 4000 MILES in a co-production with Theatre Royal Bath; a new full-length dance commission IGNIS; and the award-winning production of UNCLE VANYA by Anton Chekov, in a new translation starring Iain Glen.

Now in its fourth year, under Artistic Direction of Anda Winters, The Print Room continues to stage exciting undiscovered pieces by great writers, and create work with emerging and talented artists from all fields.

For The Print Room

Artistic Director	Anda Winters
Producer	Veronica Humphris
Assistant Producer	Isobel David
Development Officer	Julia Gale
Theatre Manager	Justine Boulton
Operations Manager	Oliver Lee
Education/Outreach Officer	Cynthia Lawford
Poetry Coordinator	Marion Manning
Bookkeeper	Andrew Michel
Master Carpenter	Rodger Pampilo
Venue Press	Julia Hallawell, Kate Morley PR

Thanks to all of our voluntary ushers.

The Print Room is a privately funded charity that receives no regular public subsidy. We are dependent on the generosity of our supporters to present our work. Thank you to all the supporters, colleagues and friends who have helped us on our journey so far. We would not be here without their kind support.

The Print Room is generously supported by:

Corporate Sponsors

Match funders and supporters of The Print Room outreach ticket scheme.

Autonomous Research, Studio Indigo

Donors: Anonymous, Aki Ando, Louisa Lane Fox, Mimi Gilligan, Jenny Hall, Bia & Mounzer Nasr

CAPITAL friends: Anonymous, Tony & Kate Best, Clive & Helene Butler, Matt Cooper, John & Jennifer Crompton, Ayelet Elstein, Lara Fares, Mike Fisher, Tom & Maarit Glocer, Ashish Goyal, Julian Granville & Louisiana Lush, Anne Herd, James Hogan, Elizabeth & Roderick Jack, Irina Knaster, Matt & Amanda McEvoy, Sir Paul & Lady Ruddock

Bold friends: Anonymous, Christiane & Bruno Boesch, Ian & Caroline Cormack, Joe & Vinah Holderness, Phil & Eliot Jacobs, Tony Mackintosh, Eloy & Letitia Michotte, Julia Rochester, Kaveh & Cora Sheibani, Rita Skinner, Vahiria Verdet-Janbon

www.the-print-room.org

Jon Fosse

THE DEAD DOGS

OBERON BOOKS
LONDON

WWW.OBERONBOOKS.COM

First published in a collection in 2011 by Oberon Books Ltd

This single edition first published in 2014 by Oberon Books Ltd
521 Caledonian Road, London N7 9RH
Tel: +44 (0) 20 7607 3637 / Fax: +44 (0) 20 7607 3629
e-mail: info@oberonbooks.com
www.oberonbooks.com

Visit www.oberonbooks.com to read more about all our books and to buy
them. You will also find features, author interviews and news of any author
events, and you can sign up for e-newsletters so that you're always first to
hear about our new releases.

Characters

THE MOTHER

THE YOUNG MAN

THE FRIEND

THE BROTHER-IN-LAW

THE SISTER

First Act

Afternoon

A living-room with a large window, two doors

THE YOUNG MAN lies on a bench with his face to the wall and THE MOTHER enters, walks over to the window

THE MOTHER
    But it's quite a nice day
    THE MOTHER looks at THE YOUNG MAN
    You could go for a walk and look for the dog
    just as well as
    lying around here
    waiting for him to come back
    of his own
    THE YOUNG MAN stays where he is
    He'll come back soon
    you'll see
    so don't worry
    Short pause
    Dogs do things like that
    they go for walks
    now and then
    It's nothing to worry about
    THE YOUNG MAN still lies there without moving
    But if it matters that much
    you should go and look for him
    then
    Short pause
    You're a grown man
    even if it's hard to believe
    so
    sit up now

and go and look for the dog
If it's that important
Pause. THE YOUNG MAN turns, looks at THE MOTHER
He'll come back
you'll see
Nothing to worry about
He's just gone for a walk

THE YOUNG MAN
He just ran
It's not like him

THE MOTHER
interrupts him
Just go and look for your dog
then
if it's that important
Short pause
It doesn't help anyone
just lying there
But we have to go to the shop
We need coffee
Perhaps you can go to the shop
short pause
and then you can
yes look for the dog
at the same time
THE YOUNG MAN sits up on the bench, nods
Yes why don't you do that

THE YOUNG MAN
But he never runs away
I was only going to walk him
as I always do
and he ran away
I called him
but he didn't stop
just kept running

He never does that

THE MOTHER

Don't be silly
Dogs do that
They take a walk now and then
Short pause

THE YOUNG MAN

Yes but

THE MOTHER

No that's enough
It's nothing to worry about
and if you do
why don't you go and look for him
Short pause
At least
it doesn't help anyone
lying there on the bench
Short pause
The dog
he'll come back
you'll see

THE YOUNG MAN

Yes

THE MOTHER

Yes come on
you can go to the shop
and then you can look for the dog
at the same time
We've got to have coffee when they arrive
Come on
She wasn't quite sure
your sister
if they were going to stay the night
Well I've bought most things

short pause
because on the rare occasion she's here
we've got to have
something nice to eat
and things
Short pause
But maybe they'll stay the night too
even if she said she couldn't
Maybe they will
She wasn't sure
But at least we've got to have coffee
I forgot to buy that
Come on
Short pause
It'll be good to see her again
It's such a long time since I've seen her

THE YOUNG MAN
But that husband of hers

THE MOTHER
Yes yes
Short pause
But you'll go up to the shop then
or are you just going to lie there
as you always do
Pause
No
I suppose I have to go up to the shop
myself then
But listen
THE MOTHER breaks off when there is a knock on the door
Oh no they can't be here already
They weren't coming till later
It can't be her
can it

*THE MOTHER goes out and THE YOUNG MAN stands up, walks
over to the window, stands and looks out and then THE MOTHER
comes in and after her comes THE FRIEND*
To THE FRIEND
Well this is a rare sight
yes
It's not often you look us up
It's been a long time
now
yes
But you live in town
and everything
don't you

THE FRIEND
I do
yes

THE MOTHER
But now you're home for a visit
Short pause
You used to
yes
you used to be here so often
well when you were a kid
Yes this is really nice

THE FRIEND
embarrassed
I just thought
breaks off

THE MOTHER
Yes this is nice
Short pause
I should've offered you coffee
but it's empty
I was on my way out the door
when you knocked

I
was going to buy coffee

THE FRIEND
Yes you've got to have coffee

THE MOTHER
But when I get back
yes
short pause
then I'll offer you coffee

THE FRIEND
looks at THE YOUNG MAN
I just thought

THE MOTHER
Interrupts
Yes it's almost like the old days
isn't it
you dropping in
And Anna's coming home tonight
yes you'll remember her
THE FRIEND nods
yes just for a brief visit
she was driving past here
so

THE FRIEND
It would be nice to talk to her
It's a

THE MOTHER
interrupts
Yes
you have to see her
Short pause
But I
yes I'll go up to the shop

then
and
and leave you alone
for a chat
THE MOTHER leaves. *THE YOUNG MAN and THE FRIEND look
at each other*

THE FRIEND

Yes I thought I'd drop in on you
See how you're going
I'm home for a visit
yes
short pause
just a brief one

THE YOUNG MAN

Yes
Short pause
So
you live in town

THE FRIEND

Yes
that's how it turned out
I had to
breaks off

THE YOUNG MAN

Yes
Pause

THE FRIEND

Money's not bad
have a bed-sitter
things could be worse
Short pause
And things are the same with you

THE YOUNG MAN

Yes not much to tell

THE FRIEND walks over to the window and looks out, then he turns to THE YOUNG MAN
Nice house he's built himself
your new neighbour

THE YOUNG MAN
Yes

THE FRIEND
Do you know him

THE YOUNG MAN
No

THE FRIEND
He doesn't talk much
is quite modest
But he's a nice guy
A little eagerly
He too has played
in a band
played the guitar
you know don't you

THE YOUNG MAN
Yes
I've heard

THE FRIEND
He did that for many years
He was supposed to be very good
But I don't think he does it anymore
Pause
And Signe
yes she lives there
down there by the sea
in her house like she used to

THE YOUNG MAN
Yes

THE FRIEND
    And she's the same old Signe

THE YOUNG MAN
    Yes she keeps to herself
    hardly ever goes out

THE FRIEND
    That's how it's been all these years

THE YOUNG MAN
    Yes

THE FRIEND
    Her house lies right on the water's edge
    I don't think I've seen another house
    so close to the sea
    When the tide's high
    it's got to reach above the foundation wall
    of the house

THE YOUNG MAN
    I don't think so
    Short pause

THE FRIEND
    But how are things with you
    You're alright

THE YOUNG MAN
    Yes thanks
    Pause

THE FRIEND
    Yes it's a long time since we've seen each other

THE YOUNG MAN
    Must be several years
    Short pause

THE FRIEND
    But isn't it boring to be here
    all the time

yes I mean
staying here at home
Short pause
The town's not all that terrific
either
really
Short pause
But
short pause
still
it's a bit better
perhaps
than hanging around here
I mean
short pause
so
yes perhaps I could get you a job in town
Short pause
Yes if you want to
of course
A little happy
I've got one waiting
you see
You know
yes they sometimes need people where I work
and then I could
yes I can help you get a bed-sitter
as well
there are several bed-sitters in the house where I live
There's often a vacant one
Short pause
So
if you want to
breaks off

THE YOUNG MAN
hesitates

No
no I don't know
Pause

THE FRIEND
But I haven't come here
to preach to you
either
Laughs shortly
You're alright

THE YOUNG MAN
shrugs his shoulders
Not bad

THE FRIEND
Yes well that's
good then
Laughs a little
Not bad
is good enough
isn't it
Pause
But listen
yes
yes perhaps we could go out on the fjord
like we used to
Yes I've still got
my old boat
Yes you remember it
THE YOUNG MAN nods
Yes of course
Short pause
Yes it was my dad's boat
And how long he had it
short pause
no I don't know
To THE YOUNG MAN

You remember the boat

THE YOUNG MAN
  Yes of course

THE FRIEND
  A fine old boat
  Short pause
  I've sanded it and looked after it well
  removed all the paint
  oiled it
  You should see how nice it is
  Short pause
  We could go out fishing

THE YOUNG MAN
  Yes
  that'd be good
  Perhaps
  We'll see

THE FRIEND
  Tomorrow maybe
  if the weather's good
  looks at THE YOUNG MAN, who doesn't answer
  Let's do that
  I'll drop in here tomorrow
  and
  and we'll see what happens

THE YOUNG MAN
  Yes
  That'd be nice

THE FRIEND
  At least
  if the weather's not too awful

THE YOUNG MAN
  It's not too awful today

THE FRIEND

But it changes all the time
Short pause
Yes
do come

THE YOUNG MAN

We'll see
Pause

THE FRIEND

Yes I just wanted to say hello
well
like the old days
yes

THE YOUNG MAN

Yes

THE FRIEND

I just wanted to drop in
yes
Pause
But where's the dog
Short pause
He's always running around
jumping about

THE YOUNG MAN

He's gone for a walk

THE FRIEND

So you dare to let him out on his own

THE YOUNG MAN

hesitates
Yes

THE FRIEND

He doesn't run away

THE YOUNG MAN

He always comes back

THE FRIEND
Yes I suppose he does

THE YOUNG MAN
Yes

THE FRIEND
I suppose he likes to run freely
go for walks

THE YOUNG MAN
Yes
Pause

THE FRIEND
Yes
I suppose
Pause
But don't you get worried about him

THE YOUNG MAN
hesitates
No

THE FRIEND
Before
yes you always had
the dog on a leash
Short pause
Yes when I picture you
you're always going around
with a dog on a leash
You and the dog
always like that
Short pause
And when I was here
it must be several years ago now
we were neighbours
childhood friends

but do we go and see each other
oh no
no do we make the effort
looks at THE YOUNG MAN
but when I was here
yes
there was always a dog here
that barked and barked
and wagged his tail
never giving us a moment's peace

THE YOUNG MAN
Yes

THE FRIEND
So I'll let you know that I won't stop
about the dog not being here
yes
that I'll let you know
okay
Pause
There's something
short pause
that's not quite right
Pause
And the dog you have now
you've had him for a long time
haven't you

THE YOUNG MAN
For many years

THE FRIEND
But you've had several dogs

THE YOUNG MAN
He's the second

THE FRIEND
So you haven't had more

THE YOUNG MAN
    No

THE FRIEND
    And I thought you'd had quite a few

THE YOUNG MAN
    One before
    who died
    he got to be about ten years
    and now this one

THE FRIEND
    You've had him a long time
    this one

THE YOUNG MAN
    Over ten years
    Short pause
    But he's in good health
    Short pause
    Yes
    a dog can live for a long time
    it depends

THE FRIEND
    No I've never had a dog

THE YOUNG MAN
    No

THE FRIEND
    I wouldn't really mind
    having a dog
    it's not that
    But it wouldn't work now
    I can't have him in my bed-sitter
    laughs shortly
    because then they'd throw me out

THE YOUNG MAN

    Yes

    Pause. THE YOUNG MAN stands and looks out the window

THE FRIEND

    Are you looking for your dog

THE YOUNG MAN

    turns to THE FRIEND

    Am I looking for my dog

THE FRIEND

    Yes

THE YOUNG MAN

    What kind of question is that

THE FRIEND

    No

    no offence

    Pause

    I just thought you were standing there looking

    for your dog

THE YOUNG MAN

    You just thought

THE FRIEND

    Yes

THE YOUNG MAN

    How did you just think that

THE FRIEND

    No reason

THE YOUNG MAN

    No reason

THE FRIEND

    But

THE YOUNG MAN
    The dog has gone for a walk
    I told you

THE FRIEND
    Yes

THE YOUNG MAN
    Yes
    needs walking

THE FRIEND
    Yes
    I suppose
    Pause
    Well I just thought
    as you always used to have him on a leash
    I mean
    Pause
    From you were just a kid
    you've always walked around with a dog on a leash
    Short pause
    As long as I can remember you've had a dog
    Always you and the dog

THE YOUNG MAN
    Yes

THE FRIEND
    You used to be so worried about the dog
    that you always had him on a leash

THE YOUNG MAN
    Yes

THE FRIEND
    But not anymore

THE YOUNG MAN
    No

THE FRIEND
fooling around
He didn't just run off then
the dog
I mean
He didn't just run away from you
Ran off
and didn't come back
when you called him

THE YOUNG MAN
Why
Why should it be like that

THE FRIEND
No I don't know
I'm just fooling around

THE YOUNG MAN
Yes
Pause

THE FRIEND
No
short pause
I just thought
that
I should drop in
yes
Short pause
It's been such a long time
Pause
And then
yes if you want to
we could go out
on the fjord
do a bit of fishing

short pause
yes like when we were kids
That'd be nice
wouldn't it

THE YOUNG MAN
Yes

THE FRIEND
If the weather's good tomorrow

THE YOUNG MAN
Yes

THE FRIEND
We'll do that then

THE YOUNG MAN
Why not

THE FRIEND
I'll come and
see you
tomorrow
if the weather's good
and there's not too much wind

THE YOUNG MAN
nods
Yes
that'll be good

THE FRIEND
We hardly ever talk these days
so
yes
breaks off. Short pause
We should keep in touch
as they say

THE YOUNG MAN
    Yes
    we should

THE FRIEND
    We'll say that then
    Short pause
    But listen
    yes it'd be good to have a chat
    with the dog
    I like dogs
    as you know

THE YOUNG MAN
    a little irritated
    But I've told you
    he's gone for a walk

THE FRIEND
    laughs a little
    Yes you and your dogs

THE YOUNG MAN
    I haven't had that many dogs
    have I

THE FRIEND
    No
    you haven't
    But always
    yes always when I've seen you walking
    along the road
    you've had a dog with you
    yes now it's the little brown one
    and earlier

THE YOUNG MAN
    interrupts
    I've only had two dogs

THE FRIEND
    First there was a white and black one

THE YOUNG MAN
    Yes

THE FRIEND
    And now the little brown one

THE YOUNG MAN
    Yes
    Pause
    I've had him for ten years
    now
    the brown one

THE FRIEND
    That long
    Short pause
    But I remember the black and white one well
    too
    You had him for a long time

THE YOUNG MAN
    Yes

THE FRIEND
    He died

THE YOUNG MAN
    Yes he grew old and died

THE FRIEND
    You must've missed him

THE YOUNG MAN
    Yes
    of course
    You know
    yes there's company in a dog
    you know

Pause

THE FRIEND

Yes I suppose you get attached to them
Pause

THE YOUNG MAN

Well yes
you do
Pause

THE FRIEND

But you
breaks off

THE YOUNG MAN

Yes
THE MOTHER enters, she holds a carrier bag in one hand

THE MOTHER

That was the shopping done
Everything done is a good deed
yes
short pause
good thing the shop's not
too far
To THE FRIEND
So now you can have some coffee
yes

THE FRIEND

I was on my way
out

THE MOTHER

Why don't you stay
It's good to see you again
And if you want coffee
I can make you a cup

THE FRIEND
Well thanks
but
yes
I'm
leaving
now
yes

THE MOTHER
But you'll have to drop in again

THE FRIEND
We've been talking about that

THE YOUNG MAN
to THE FRIEND
We'll talk
then
short pause
tomorrow
THE YOUNG MAN turns to the window again, stands and looks out, then he turns to THE MOTHER

THE MOTHER
to THE FRIEND
Well yes
Pause
It was nice of you to drop in
yes

THE FRIEND
Yes
I thought I should

THE MOTHER
That's good
yes

THE FRIEND
> *to THE YOUNG MAN*
> Yes I'll be
> going
> then
> And we'll talk
> *To THE MOTHER*
> Yes we thought
> we'd go out on the fjord
> do a bit of fishing
> maybe

THE MOTHER
> Yes why don't you
> *To THE YOUNG MAN*
> You should go fishing
> yes

THE YOUNG MAN
> Perhaps

THE MOTHER
> Yes well

THE FRIEND
> I'll be
> leaving
> then

THE MOTHER
> Yes you take care now
> and thanks for dropping in

THE YOUNG MAN
> See you

THE FRIEND
> We'll talk
> *THE FRIEND leaves*

THE MOTHER
sighs
Oh well
Pause
At least I've got some coffee in the house
Short pause
And that's good
Short pause
And now it won't be too long
before she's here
yes
your sister
THE MOTHER looks at THE YOUNG MAN, then she looks down,
stands like that for a while

THE YOUNG MAN
You didn't see the dog

THE MOTHER
Did I see the dog

THE YOUNG MAN
Yes

THE MOTHER
No I didn't see the dog
Quite short pause
Nice of him to drop in
Leif
It's been a long time
And you
yes
yes you must go out on the fjord with him

THE YOUNG MAN
Yes

THE MOTHER
Of course you must

THE YOUNG MAN
Yes
Pause

THE MOTHER
He's just gone for a walk
the dog
And she'll soon arrive
your sister
Short pause
But you've never really liked him
have you
yes her husband

THE YOUNG MAN
No
never
Do you like him
then

THE MOTHER
Like and like
Short pause
There's nothing wrong with him
is there
Pause
Oh well
Pause
But
yes
short pause
it was nice that Leif
dropped in
yes
It's been a long time since you've had a chat
with him

THE YOUNG MAN
> Many years
> *Pause*
> But that he's
> coming here

THE MOTHER
> You'll have to try to make the best of it

THE YOUNG MAN
> Make the best of it

THE MOTHER
> There isn't much else you can do
> He is married to your sister
> *Long pause*
> But listen
> you haven't seen the dog

THE YOUNG MAN
> Have I seen the dog
> Why do you ask about that

THE MOTHER
> No nothing

THE YOUNG MAN
> What is it
> Why do you ask

THE MOTHER
> No nothing

THE YOUNG MAN
> Just say it
> Say what you're thinking

THE MOTHER
> *hesitates*
> No

THE YOUNG MAN

    Yes say it

THE MOTHER

    No it's nothing

THE YOUNG MAN

    Yes say it

THE MOTHER

    I was just asking

THE YOUNG MAN goes and lies down on the bench, lies and stares ahead and THE MOTHER goes out with the carrier bag and he turns, lies with his face to the wall

Lights down. Black

II

Evening the same day. THE MOTHER stands and looks out of the window and THE YOUNG MAN lies on the bench and stares straight ahead

THE MOTHER
    looks at THE YOUNG MAN
    But it's strange they don't come
    Short pause
    They should've been here a long time ago
    And at least they could've called
    Short pause
    And you're just lying there
    now you've been lying there all day
    Pause
    You can't do that
    just lying there like that
    young man like you
    You could've gone to look
    for the dog
    when he ran away
    Instead you went to lie on the bench
    Short pause
    And at least they could've called
    if something had come up
    yes
    yes I do think that

THE YOUNG MAN
    turns and looks at THE MOTHER
    I don't understand why the dog isn't coming back

THE MOTHER
    No it is a bit strange
    THE MOTHER goes to THE YOUNG MAN, stops

THE YOUNG MAN

Yes

THE YOUNG MAN sits up on the bench

THE MOTHER

But it's just a dog

yes

THE YOUNG MAN

Just a dog

THE MOTHER

Yes just a dog

Short pause

And if you're worried about him

you'll have to do something

go and look for him

You can't just

breaks off, quite short pause

No

Pause

And then that sister of yours

why isn't she coming

THE YOUNG MAN

It's best if they don't come

I can't stand that husband of hers

Short pause

I haven't liked him from the moment

I set eyes on him

THE MOTHER

But we're family

we have to live together

the best we can

THE YOUNG MAN

But I can't bear him

THE MOTHER

No but
Short pause
He's just
yes an ordinary man
him too

THE YOUNG MAN

Are they bringing the girls

THE MOTHER

No they're at his mum's place
They've been to a wedding
a friend of his
I told you

THE YOUNG MAN

Yes
Short pause

THE MOTHER

But
listens
yes isn't that a car
THE MOTHER walks to the window, looks out
Yes there they are
That's a relief
THE YOUNG MAN stands up
What a relief they're finally here
Short pause
And it's so long since she was last here
your sister
Short pause
And he's not all that bad
I tell you
your brother-in-law
It's not
breaks off

THE YOUNG MAN
>No
>*Short pause*

THE MOTHER
>I should go out
>welcome them
>*Short pause*

THE YOUNG MAN
>Yes
>*There is a knock and just afterwards THE SISTER enters*

THE SISTER
>Yes finally we're here
>It took its time

THE MOTHER
>Good to see you
>I was beginning to worry about you

THE SISTER
>Yes
>yes I know
>But now
>yes we're here
>now

THE MOTHER
>Yes finally
>*Short pause*
>And you had a good trip

THE SISTER
>Yes
>we did
>*To THE YOUNG MAN*
>Nice to see you

THE MOTHER

I'm glad you've arrived
THE BROTHER-IN-LAW enters, he carries a bag

THE BROTHER-IN-LAW

to THE MOTHER
Yes
smiles
finally we're here
Yes it took it's time
this

THE MOTHER

Yes I've been waiting and waiting

THE BROTHER-IN-LAW

Well you know
he looks quickly at THE YOUNG MAN, then at THE MOTHER again
we got to bed pretty late
and then we didn't get up early
either
yes and then there was one thing and another

THE MOTHER

Yes of course
Pause

THE BROTHER-IN-LAW

And here everything's the same
THE BROTHER-IN-LAW looks at THE YOUNG MAN
Everything's the same with you
Short pause
Nothing new

THE YOUNG MAN

No
same as always

THE BROTHER-IN-LAW
>*to THE MOTHER*
>Yes it was good to get here
>*Short pause*
>It was a long trip

THE MOTHER
>*to THE SISTER*
>Did you enjoy the wedding

THE SISTER
>Yes

THE BROTHER-IN-LAW
>It was a big party
>yes

THE MOTHER
>There were many guests

THE BROTHER-IN-LAW
>You

THE SISTER
>Yes there were many people

THE BROTHER-IN-LAW
>*to THE YOUNG MAN*
>And you're alright
>then

THE YOUNG MAN
>Yes

THE MOTHER
>*to THE BROTHER-IN-LAW*
>So it was a nice wedding
>then

THE BROTHER IN LAW
to THE YOUNG MAN
Everything's the same old
is it

THE YOUNG MAN
Yes

THE MOTHER
to THE BROTHER-IN-LAW
And everything was nice and proper

THE SISTER
to THE MOTHER
Yes
on the whole

THE MOTHER
There was dancing and things

THE BROTHER-IN-LAW
Yes into the early hours

THE MOTHER
And they
got married
They already have two children
haven't they

THE SISTER
And they were at the wedding
The girl was a bride's maid

THE MOTHER
Yes that's how it is these days

THE BROTHER-IN-LAW
to THE YOUNG MAN
It was a nice wedding

THE MOTHER
That's good to hear

THE BROTHER-IN-LAW

But have you spoken to your new neighbour
lately
yes I know him a bit
you see
from before

THE MOTHER

answers before he has finished
No
only when we meet
yes
at the shop
or something like that
a couple of words
perhaps
He's not exactly chatty
Short pause
He's a quiet man mostly

THE BROTHER-IN-LAW

Yes I suppose
he is
But he's built himself a fine house

THE MOTHER

Yes

THE BROTHER-IN-LAW

And doesn't he have two girls

THE MOTHER

Two nice girls

THE BROTHER-IN-LAW

I'd be good to talk to him for old time's sake

THE MOTHER

Why don't you go over and have a chat

THE BROTHER-IN-LAW

    Yes

    that'd be good

THE MOTHER

    Why don't you do that

    then

THE BROTHER-IN-LAW

    I know him a bit from before

    you see

    we'd see each other now and then

    once upon a time

    It's a few years ago

    now

    He's a nice fellow

    very quiet

    To THE YOUNG MAN

    Have you spoken to him

    THE YOUNG MAN shakes his head

    Still to THE YOUNG MAN

    I know him a bit

    you see

    yes

THE MOTHER

    Yes

THE BROTHER-IN-LAW

    Oh yes

    Short pause

THE MOTHER

    But let me get you some coffee

    and a bite to eat

    maybe

THE SISTER

    Yes that'd be good

THE BROTHER-IN-LAW
>I'd like
>that

THE MOTHER
>Yes it was a close call
>with the coffee
>I discovered just before the shop closed
>that I didn't have any coffee left
>but I got there
>just in time

THE SISTER
>Yes then we'd have had to go
>without coffee

THE MOTHER
>We'd have coped with that
>too

THE BROTHER-IN-LAW
>*to THE YOUNG MAN*
>But what have you done with the dog

THE YOUNG MAN
>He's outside

THE BROTHER-IN-LAW
>You dare to let him out alone
>yes
>I'd love to have a dog
>myself
>but your sister doesn't want to
>I've always like dogs
>I had a dog when I was a boy
>*Short pause*
>But they had to take him
>he bit a kid

THE YOUNG MAN
    Yes

THE BROTHER-IN-LAW
    But she doesn't want us to have a dog
    yes your sister
    So no more dogs for me
    Quite short pause
    He's outside the house
    your dog

THE YOUNG MAN
    Think so

THE BROTHER-IN-LAW
    I suppose he likes being outside

THE YOUNG MAN
    Yes

THE BROTHER-IN-LAW
    to THE MOTHER
    And otherwise everything's the same

THE MOTHER
    Yes it's all calm and quiet

THE BROTHER-IN-LAW
    Yes I suppose
    it is
    THE BROTHER-IN-LAW walks to the window, looks out

THE MOTHER
    To THE SISTER
    It's getting very late
    so I suppose you'll stay till tomorrow

THE SISTER
    Yes
    I suppose that's best
    The girls can stay with their grandma

for a while tomorrow
But she was going to the doctor around midday
so we have to come for them before that

THE MOTHER

It's nice
that you're staying the night
Short pause
But it would've been nice to see the girls too

THE SISTER

We'll all have to come for a visit soon

THE BROTHER-IN-LAW

There
yes I see your neighbour down on the road
I think I'll go and have a few words
with him
yes
the way
I used to

THE SISTER

Yes

THE BROTHER-IN-LAW

It's a long time since we've had a chat

THE MOTHER

And you mustn't be too long
I'm getting the meal ready
now

THE BROTHER-IN-LAW

No
just a short chat
THE BROTHER-IN-LAW leaves, takes his bag with him. Pause

THE YOUNG MAN
    to THE SISTER
    All's well then

THE SISTER
    Yes well it's busy
    two kids
    and a full-time job
    but
    yes all's well
    And what about you

THE YOUNG MAN
    Yes
    well

THE MOTHER
    Yes all's well
    with us
    Pause

THE SISTER
    It's a long time since I've been home now

THE MOTHER
    Yes it's nice to see you again

THE SISTER
    We're so busy
    you know

THE MOTHER
    And the girls are good

THE SISTER
    Yes they grow and blossom

THE MOTHER
    That's good
    yes
    Pause

THE SISTER
    It's incredible how quickly time flies

THE MOTHER
    Yes they're soon grown-ups
    your girls
    are

THE SISTER
    Don't talk about it

THE MOTHER
    They can soon come here
    to visit their grandma
    on their own
    the two of them

THE SISTER
    I suppose they could
    But I don't really like the thought of it
    Laughs
    Yes not the thought that they're coming here
    but thinking about how big they've grown
    I mean
    Pause

THE MOTHER
    I should get us something to eat
    shouldn't I
    Pause

THE SISTER
    Yes
    everything's the same here

THE YOUNG MAN
    Yes
    Pause

THE SISTER
    Do you play the guitar a lot

THE YOUNG MAN
    hesitates
    No

THE MOTHER
    No less and less these days

THE SISTER
    That's all you ever used to do

THE MOTHER
    He played all the time
    It got to be too much to listen to
    to tell the truth
    THE MOTHER laughs shortly

THE SISTER
    Don't you like it anymore

THE YOUNG MAN
    hesitates
    No

THE SISTER
    But you were so good

THE YOUNG MAN
    Not all that good
    Pause

THE MOTHER
    And he's got no one to play with anymore

THE SISTER
    Oh I see
    I suppose it gets boring to play on your own
    But surely you play now and then
    THE YOUNG MAN shakes his head

THE MOTHER

>He's sold the guitar

THE SISTER

>You'd have been pretty broke
>then
>I'd have thought

THE YOUNG MAN

>No I
>*breaks off, quite short pause*

THE MOTHER

>But Leif
>his friend
>his childhood friend
>was here today
>Yes you'll remember him

THE SISTER

>Yes

THE MOTHER

>He's home for a visit

THE SISTER

>He works in town
>doesn't
>he

THE MOTHER

>Yes
>*Short pause*

THE SISTER

>*to THE YOUNG MAN*
>And everything's good with him
>yes with Leif

THE YOUNG MAN
Think so
Short pause

THE MOTHER
Yes it was nice of him to drop in
It's not often we see
him
either

THE SISTER
He doesn't come home often

THE MOTHER
No
just now and then

THE SISTER
Yes I suppose it's been a while
since he set foot in this house

THE MOTHER
Years

THE SISTER
to THE YOUNG MAN
So it was good to see him again then

THE YOUNG MAN
Yes

THE SISTER
Is he coming back

THE YOUNG MAN
Perhaps we'll go for
yes
yes go out on the fjord tomorrow
do some fishing

THE SISTER
He has a boat

THE YOUNG MAN
His dad's old boat

THE SISTER
Yes he got it when his dad died

THE YOUNG MAN
Yes
Pause

THE SISTER
thinks briefly
Yes I remember it
Short pause
His Dad was often fishing
wasn't he

THE YOUNG MAN
Yes
Pause

THE SISTER
And now he is fishing
the son is

THE YOUNG MAN
Now and then I suppose

THE MOTHER
When he's at home
short pause
but he's not often here
He works in town
yes
Short pause
No I should go and get some dinner
THE MOTHER leaves. Pause

THE YOUNG MAN
   You're staying the night

THE SISTER
   Looks like it
   Short pause
   There's fish in the fjord

THE YOUNG MAN
   Think so

THE SISTER
   Sure to be
   Pause
   You like to fish

THE YOUNG MAN
   A bit

THE SISTER
   At least you used to like it
   when you were a kid

THE YOUNG MAN
   Yes
   Pause

THE SISTER
   So you don't play the guitar anymore

THE YOUNG MAN
   no
   it's been a long time since I played
   now

THE SISTER
   You didn't want to anymore

THE YOUNG MAN
   No

THE SISTER
>And you didn't have anyone to play with

THE YOUNG MAN
>That too
>*Short pause*

THE SISTER
>But you shouldn't have stopped playing the guitar

THE YOUNG MAN
>Yes

THE SISTER
>You were so good

THE YOUNG MAN
>Not all that good

THE SISTER
>Yes

THE YOUNG MAN
>I didn't like it anymore
>*Pause*

THE SISTER
>But you've got your dog
>*Laughs*
>No what am I saying
>Aren't you worried about him
>when he's walking
>yes running around
>as he likes
>*THE MOTHER enters*

THE MOTHER
>Dinner's soon ready
>*Pause*
>*To THE SISTER*
>But your husband

short pause
he'll be here soon

THE SISTER
Well he knew we were eating soon
THE SISTER goes to the window, looks out, then she turns to THE MOTHER
He's standing down on the road
talking to him
short pause
yes to him
to that new neighbour of yours

THE MOTHER
Yes they knew each other
from before
those two

THE SISTER
They're chatting away
Short pause
I think they used to see each other a lot
at one time
I think he said
THE SISTER laughs briefly

THE MOTHER
Yes
Short pause

THE SISTER
Don't you like him
your new neighbour

THE MOTHER
There's nothing wrong with him
Pause

THE SISTER
　No

THE MOTHER
　But well I don't know him

THE SISTER
　No
　Pause
　And here everything
　is the same old
　yes

THE MOTHER
　Nothing much happens
　no
　Short pause
　But let's hope
　he'll come soon
　your husband
　Dinner's ready
　THE SISTER looks out through the window

THE SISTER
　Yes he's coming
　At least I can't see him

THE MOTHER
　Good

THE SISTER
　I could do with a bite to eat

THE MOTHER
　Yes it was nice to see you again
　We don't see each other
　very often

THE SISTER
　Not often at all

THE MOTHER
>And the girls
>it would've been nice to see
>them too

THE SISTER
>We must come back
>soon
>and then they'll have to come too

THE MOTHER
>Yes they must
>*Pause*

THE SISTER
>*to THE YOUNG MAN*
>It was a surprise that you've stopped playing the guitar

THE MOTHER
>Yes

THE SISTER
>I'd never have thought it
>*Short pause*
>You and that guitar
>you were almost inseparable
>*Short pause*
>And you were so good
>I thought you were incredibly good
>I did
>you could play anything
>if you heard a song
>you could play the tune
>immediately

THE YOUNG MAN
>No
>I could only do that now and then

THE SISTER
    But still

THE YOUNG MAN
    I wasn't very good

THE SISTER
    Don't say that

THE YOUNG MAN
    I wasn't exactly bad
    but a bit bad
    at least

THE SISTER
    But you liked it
    yes playing the guitar

THE YOUNG MAN
    Yes
    short pause
    perhaps
    in a way
    but then
    short pause
    yes then I didn't like it anymore
    I plainly disliked it
    I couldn't stand it

THE SISTER
    Oh well then

THE YOUNG MAN
    I didn't want to play anymore

THE SISTER
    But

THE MOTHER
    We're eating soon

THE SISTER
He'll be coming soon

THE MOTHER
Yes he must come now

THE SISTER
walks to the window, looks out
I can't see him

THE MOTHER
Good
Pause

THE SISTER
to THE YOUNG MAN
Yes when I think about you
it's a dog and a guitar I'm seeing
Pause. THE BROTHER-IN-LAW enters

THE BROTHER-IN-LAW
a little out of breath, to THE YOUNG MAN
Listen
yes
short pause
yes
short pause

THE MOTHER
What is it

THE BROTHER-IN-LAW
Yes
you must
yes go out

THE MOTHER
Go out

THE BROTHER-IN-LAW
Yes there's
short pause
yes something's lying
there
outside the door

THE MOTHER
Something's lying outside the door

THE BROTHER-IN-LAW
In the yard
yes there outside the entrance door
in the yard
It's
breaks off

THE SISTER
Something's lying
What do you mean

THE BROTHER-IN-LAW
Yes
THE BROTHER-IN-LAW looks a little helplessly at THE SISTER
Yes

THE MOTHER
Something's lying

THE BROTHER-IN-LAW
Yes
short pause
but
Pause. THE YOUNG MAN goes outside
But
yes it's awful
but
yes
yes his dog

THE SISTER
His dog

THE BROTHER-IN-LAW
Yes
short pause
yes it's
breaks off

THE MOTHER
What is it with the dog

THE BROTHER-IN-LAW
It's dead
Short pause

THE SISTER
Well he was old

THE MOTHER
Yes

THE SISTER
But he was so fond of that dog
Short pause

THE MOTHER
Very fond of him

THE SISTER
He's always been so fond of dogs

THE MOTHER
Almost too fond

THE SISTER
Yes it's as if
well dogs

THE MOTHER
Since he was a little kid he's been fond of them

THE SISTER
I've never quite understood it

THE MOTHER
No

THE BROTHER-IN-LAW
But
yes

THE SISTER
Always him and a dog

THE MOTHER
It's almost
too much

THE BROTHER-IN-LAW
But

THE SISTER
No how awful that he's dead
his dog
Short pause
He's had him for so long

THE MOTHER
Ten years
Fifteen perhaps

THE SISTER
He
breaks off. Pause

THE BROTHER-IN-LAW
Yes
short pause
yes the dog was old
but
yes
quite short pause

yes

He seems to have shot it

the neighbour

THE SISTER

Он shot the dog

THE BROTHER-IN-LAW

Yes

yes

it seems it just happened

And he regretted it of course

He just got so angry

quite short pause

yes

he regretted it

didn't know what to do

was scared about what he'd say

and then

yes

then he put the dog in a plastic bag

well he had to

yes he had to put him some place

of course

And then

well

THE SISTER

In a plastic bag

a black plastic bag

THE BROTHER-IN-LAW

And he wondered if he should bury the dog

or

And then

yes I thought

yes I said I could take him up here

That that was best
But I don't know
Perhaps
breaks off

THE SISTER

exasperated
No
That's awful
It's as if everything goes wrong
for him
That was the dog
that was his

THE BROTHER-IN-LAW

Yes he really regretted it too
Didn't know what to say

THE SISTER

But he can get a new dog

THE BROTHER-IN-LAW

He shouldn't have done it
he said
but
yes
the dog
yes it had
well been shitting in his garden several times
and then
yes today
it'd closed its mouth around the arm of one of his
daughters
She wanted to play with the dog
And then
well
it didn't break the skin

but
yes you could see the marks from the teeth
in her skin
And he got so scared
he said
And very angry
Short pause
Yes you know how it is
when there's something with the kids

THE SISTER
Yes

THE BROTHER-IN-LAW
Yes you worry about the kids
of course
And if something happens to them
then
yes
short pause
and to me
yes
I remember
when I was a kid
and they took my dog

THE SISTER
You've often talked about it

THE BROTHER-IN-LAW
I still haven't quite got over it
Pause

THE MOTHER
So he's shot the dog
has he
yes

THE BROTHER-IN-LAW
Yes
Short pause
And perhaps I shouldn't have
well taken him back here

THE SISTER
But still
No it's unheard of

THE MOTHER
Well
then

THE BROTHER-IN-LAW
That's how it is

THE SISTER
And he was so fond of that dog
No it's really unheard of

THE BROTHER-IN-LAW
He was fond of him
yes

THE SISTER
No it's unheard of

THE MOTHER
So that's how it is
yes

Lights down. Black

Second Act

III

The morning after. THE YOUNG MAN is looking out of the window and THE MOTHER is looking at him.

THE MOTHER

Don't stand there and look at it
yes at that grave you've dug
or whatever I should call it
you could've buried your dog somewhere else
not right outside the living-room window
THE MOTHER laughs exasperatedly
No it's unheard of
bury the dog
in the middle of the night
and then bury him
right outside the living-room window

THE YOUNG MAN

There weren't a lot of places

THE MOTHER

But
not right there
Short pause
And you don't need to stand there all the time
and look down on the grave
Yes

THE YOUNG MAN

No
Pause

THE MOTHER
So don't stand there
then

THE YOUNG MAN
Why can't I stand here

THE MOTHER
I don't like it

THE YOUNG MAN
You don't like it

THE MOTHER
No I don't like it

THE YOUNG MAN
What's wrong with me standing here

THE MOTHER
I don't like it
I said

THE YOUNG MAN
But I like it

THE MOTHER
You like it

THE YOUNG MAN
Well I'm standing here

THE MOTHER
So stand there
then
Pause. THE SISTER enters and THE MOTHER looks at her, shakes her head

THE SISTER
Yes I suppose we should get going soon

THE MOTHER
>*to THE SISTER*
>He's just standing
>there

THE SISTER
>Yes
>*Pause*
>Yes well
>he is
>*Pause*
>Yes we
>*quite short pause*
>I suppose we should get home
>got to pick up the kids
>my mother-in-law's going to the doctor

THE MOTHER
>Are you in such a rush

THE SISTER
>Yes we've got to pick up the kids in good time before
>twelve o'clock

THE MOTHER
>Yes
>*Pause*

THE SISTER
>Yes
>*short pause*
>if only he could come now
>so we

THE MOTHER
>*breaks off*
>*To THE YOUNG MAN*
>But come over here
>Don't just stand there
>Talk to your sister

before she leaves

THE SISTER

to THE YOUNG MAN
Yes I've got to go
in a minute
short pause
if only he could come

THE MOTHER

But he went for a walk
your husband did

THE SISTER

Yes well
and of course he's not coming back
in time
he said he was only going for a short walk
down to the fjord
down to the shore
Short pause
Why isn't he coming

THE MOTHER

He'll be here in a minute

THE SISTER

But he said he was only going down to the shore
going for a short walk
And then he's away for so long

THE MOTHER

He'll be here in a minute
you'll see

THE SISTER

He couldn't have forgotten himself totally
*THE SISTER looks at the window where THE YOUNG MAN stands
and looks out*
To THE YOUNG MAN
Can you see him

THE YOUNG MAN doesn't answer
To THE MOTHER
It's always like this
Pause. THE SISTER walks over to the window, looks out
Yes it's nice here
when it doesn't rain
at least
The fjord and the mountains
It's a nice day
yes
short pause
and the fjord is almost dead calm
Short pause
And there
on the road there
there he is
your childhood friend
that
yes Leif

THE YOUNG MAN
Yes

THE SISTER
Perhaps he's coming up here
Short pause
No he seems to be walking past

THE YOUNG MAN
Yes
Pause

THE SISTER
It's a nice day
so today you could
yes you and he
that Leif
could go out fishing
Didn't you have a date for that

THE MOTHER
  Of course you do
  And Leif
  he walked past down on the road

THE SISTER
  Yes

THE MOTHER
  Yes
  quite short pause
  it's a nice day
  Short pause
  It's in the winter especially
  at its darkest
  yes then it can be hard here
  But spring's nice
  And the autumn can finally be nice
  as well

THE SISTER
  to THE MOTHER
  Yes
  that's how it is
  But
  he has to come now
  that husband of mine
  yes if he doesn't come soon
  I'll have to go and look for him

THE YOUNG MAN
  I think he went up to the neighbour's

THE SISTER
Did he go into the neighbour's place
That doesn't surprise me

THE YOUNG MAN
Yes a while ago

THE MOTHER
He'll be here soon
He knows we've got to be back in time
Pause

THE SISTER
But why isn't he coming
Pause
Yes it was terrible about the dog
but you've dug a nice grave
for him

THE MOTHER
Yes hasn't he

THE YOUNG MAN
Had to do that
I had to have him somewhere

THE MOTHER
Have him somewhere
well
now

THE SISTER
Oh well
Pause. THE SISTER looks out of the window
There he is
yes
thank god
Yes
it looks like he's been to your new neighbour
he's
standing there in the yard

there outside his house
yes it's a nice house he's built himself
your new neighbour

THE MOTHER

Yes

THE SISTER

But he looks as if he's got plenty of time
he doesn't seem to want to hurry back
exactly
I suppose I'll have to go and get him

THE MOTHER

He'll be here in a minute
you'll see

THE SISTER

And now there's a car driving
up to the neighbour's
no
to THE MOTHER
no I'll go and get him

THE MOTHER

Yes
yes you'd better

THE SISTER

He can't just stand there in the yard
when we should've left a long time ago
Short pause
And now someone else has arrived that he can talk to
the one in that car
No he's got to come now
No I'll go and get him

THE MOTHER

Yes
why don't you

THE SISTER

 Yes

 I suppose I should

 THE SISTER goes out and THE MOTHER walks out on the floor,
 stops, stands and looks down. Pause

THE MOTHER

 looks at THE YOUNG MAN

 But don't stand there

 you can't stand there at the window

 and look down on that grave

 Come and have some coffee

 You haven't even had any coffee

 today

THE YOUNG MAN

 No

 I don't want any coffee

 Long pause

THE MOTHER

 Don't take it so hard about the dog

 It's just a dog

 Short pause

 There's freshly made coffee in the kitchen

THE YOUNG MAN

 I don't want any

 I said

THE MOTHER

 Don't think about the dog

 anymore

 Pause

 You can get a new dog

 THE MOTHER walks over to the window, stands and looks out

THE YOUNG MAN

 I don't want a new dog

THE MOTHER

But look at that car
isn't it
yes
yes the doctor's car

THE YOUNG MAN
How should I know

THE MOTHER
I think it is
I think the doctor has
yes one of those
big
blue
cars
That was the one
arriving just now
wasn't it
No I don't know
I suppose it could be any car

THE YOUNG MAN
Yes
Pause. THE MOTHER walks away from the window.
But listen
come over here
have something to eat
have a cup of coffee
don't just stand there
please

THE YOUNG MAN
I'm just standing here
do you mind

THE MOTHER
No
but
short pause

don't think about the dog
anymore
think about something else
have something to eat
go for a walk
short pause
and then
yes later today
you and Leif can go out on the fjord
do a bit of fishing

THE YOUNG MAN
Why can't I just stand here
Am I doing something wrong
Am I bothering you

THE MOTHER
Not you're not
but
breaks off. THE MOTHER walks over to the window again, looks out
And now
yes that car
there's yet another car there now
Wonder what's up
And Anna

THE YOUNG MAN
Yes

THE MOTHER
I can't see her
Short pause
Not her husband either
Pause
It arrived just now
too
the other car

THE YOUNG MAN

Yes

THE MOTHER walks away from the window, looks at THE
YOUNG MAN

But come now

come and have some coffee

Long pause

THE YOUNG MAN

Now they're coming

THE MOTHER walks over to the window again, looks out

THE MOTHER

But what's up with them

THE YOUNG MAN

With them

THE MOTHER

Yes them

breaks off

What's wrong

Very long pause. THE SISTER comes back followed by THE
BROTHER IN-LAW

THE SISTER

out of breath

It's dreadful

so dreadful

THE MOTHER and THE YOUNG MAN look at her

THE BROTHER-IN-LAW

out of breath

Last night

THE MOTHER

In suspense

Yes

THE SISTER nods

THE SISTER

Last night

THE BROTHER-IN-LAW
Yes
Pause
He
pause
yes
he's dead
yes your neighbour

THE SISTER
It's so dreadful

THE BROTHER-IN-LAW
Yes he
shakes his head in disbelief
yes he
ooh
yes
no
it
yes he
he
sighs
they say he was
yes
stabbed to death

THE SISTER
It's
breaks off

THE BROTHER-IN-LAW
Yes
and
yes
they say it was
yes his daughter
she found him
yes

the youngest one
and
breaks off

THE SISTER
It's so dreadful
Short pause

THE MOTHER
It
yes
breaks off

THE BROTHER-IN-LAW
I
quite short pause
yes I
breaks off

THE SISTER
It's unheard of
I don't believe it
Short pause
The doctor's there
And the police
yes
so
And his wife
they say she's not
at home
just the daughters
yes
and the youngest one
breaks off
It's so
breaks off

THE MOTHER
No it

It
as if searching for something to say
It

THE BROTHER-IN-LAW
And he
young
two little girls

THE MOTHER
It
short pause
yes

THE SISTER
It's true
I can't believe it
I
breaks off. THE SISTER walks over to the window, looks out

THE MOTHER
It's
breaks off

THE YOUNG MAN
Yes

THE SISTER
I don't understand it
It can't have happened

THE BROTHER-IN-LAW
No it's unheard of

THE SISTER
Yes
Short pause

THE YOUNG MAN
to THE SISTER
Are you sure

THE SISTER

Yes yes
Short pause
But I can't
breaks off

THE MOTHER
No it
breaks off

THE SISTER
No

THE MOTHER
No it can't be true
Pause. THE YOUNG MAN looks at THE MOTHER
No it's unbelievable
Pause
I don't believe it
It's unheard of
Short pause

THE YOUNG MAN
No it isn't
breaks off

THE MOTHER
It's too awful

THE YOUNG MAN
Yes

THE MOTHER
I can't believe
that he
is dead
two little girls
two little kids
little girls

THE YOUNG MAN
Yes

THE SISTER
> Yes it's unbelievable
> So dreadful
> *Pause*

THE MOTHER
> Yes
> *To THE BROTHER-IN-LAW*
> And it was one of the girls
> who found him

THE BROTHER-IN-LAW
> The youngest one
> yes
> *Short pause*
> Yes
> *Short pause*
> The wife's away
> she's doing something or other
> and then he's lying there in his bed
> *short pause*
> yes
> blood
> blood everywhere
> *Pause*

THE MOTHER
> Yes
> *Long pause*

THE SISTER
> *as if suddenly occurring to her*
> *To THE BROTHER-IN-LAW*
> But we
> yes will have to
> we'll have to
> yes
> or

THE BROTHER-IN-LAW
Yes

THE SISTER
Yes

THE BROTHER-IN-LAW
Yes there's nothing
well
there's nothing we can
short pause
do
quite short pause
anyway

THE SISTER
No
Short pause
And we're already
late
so we must
breaks off

THE MOTHER
You can't leave
Not now

THE SISTER
No
but
we should
breaks off

THE BROTHER-IN-LAW
Yes my mother
yes

THE SISTER
to THE MOTHER
So I suppose we'll
breaks off

THE MOTHER
> Yes
> *Pause*
> No this
> *breaks off. Short pause*

THE SISTER
> I'd like to
> *breaks off. Looks at THE BROTHER-IN-LAW*
> Yes
> *Short pause*
> *To THE MOTHER*
> I would really like to say
> but
> *breaks off*

THE MOTHER
> And his girls

THE SISTER
> Yes

THE MOTHER
> What about them

THE BROTHER-IN-LAW
> Well they're down with
> that woman
> *breaks off*

THE MOTHER
> Yes with Signe
> yes
> *Short pause*
> And his wife
> she
> *short pause*
> she
> yes she
> *breaks off*

THE SISTER
    No
    short pause
    but we

THE MOTHER
    I should go down
    yes to Signe
    perhaps I can
    breaks off
    To THE YOUNG MAN
    Do you want to come

THE YOUNG MAN
    No

THE MOTHER
    I should
    breaks off. THE YOUNG MAN walks around a little, looks at THE
    MOTHER. Pause

THE BROTHER-IN-LAW
    I don't understand it

THE SISTER
    Me neither
    Pause

THE BROTHER-IN-LAW
    I think
    breaks off. THE BROTHER-IN-LAW walks over to the window,
    stands and looks out.
    Yes now there's an ambulance outside the house

THE SISTER
    Yes
    Short pause

THE BROTHER-IN-LAW
    And there they're coming out with a stretcher
    Now they're carrying him out
    He's covered

yes
of course

THE MOTHER
And what's going to happen
with his girls
Someone has to look after them
I should
breaks off

THE SISTER
Yes

THE MOTHER
Yes I
breaks off

THE YOUNG MAN
Yes someone has to look after them

THE SISTER
Yes

THE YOUNG MAN
They can't be alone
short pause
now that the father
breaks off

THE BROTHER-IN-LAW
And there was
an awful lot of blood
so
short pause
well it
breaks off, short pause

THE YOUNG MAN
Yes
Pause

THE BROTHER-IN-LAW
> They're putting him in the car now
> sliding the stretcher into the ambulance

THE YOUNG MAN
> Yes
> *Pause*

THE MOTHER
> Yes
> *Short pause*
> It's
> *breaks off*

THE SISTER
> I
> *breaks off*

THE MOTHER
> It's
> *breaks off*

THE BROTHER-IN-LAW
> Now the ambulance
> is driving off
> *Short pause*

THE YOUNG MAN
> It's
> *breaks off. Long pause*

THE SISTER
> No we must
> *breaks off*

THE BROTHER-IN-LAW
> *continues*
> yes we must leave
> let's
> *breaks off, short pause*

THE SISTER
Yes
Short pause

THE MOTHER
It's
breaks off

THE YOUNG MAN
Yes
Pause

THE MOTHER
I
no I don't know
I
breaks off

THE YOUNG MAN
No
THE SISTER walks to the door

THE MOTHER
Yes do you have to leave

THE SISTER
Yes I suppose we
breaks off

THE BROTHER-IN-LAW
I suppose we'll have to

THE YOUNG MAN
Yes
To THE SISTER and THE BROTHER-IN-LAW
You're leaving

THE SISTER
Yes I suppose we must
THE SISTER looks at THE YOUNG MAN, then she looks at THE BROTHER-IN-LAW
You mustn't just stand there and look out of the window

we don't have time for that
We must leave

THE BROTHER-IN-LAW
Yes
Pause

THE SISTER
But why are you just standing there
yes
I'm talking to you
and you're not answering
Short pause
But come now
Pause
Come

THE BROTHER-IN-LAW
turns to THE YOUNG MAN
Is it your dog you've buried in the garden
there
THE YOUNG MAN nods. Pause
You've buried your dog in the garden

THE YOUNG MAN
I had to
quite short pause
didn't I
Long pause

THE SISTER
No we must leave

THE BROTHER-IN-LAW
I suppose we must

THE SISTER
Are you coming

THE BROTHER-IN-LAW
Yes

THE SISTER

We'll call you

THE MOTHER

Yes you must

breaks off. Short pause. THE SISTER and THE BROTHER-IN-LAW
walk out and THE YOUNG MAN goes and lies down on the bench
and looks straight ahead of him while THE MOTHER walks over
to the window, stands and looks out. Quite long pause

THE MOTHER

The car's leaving now

Short pause

And it

breaks off. THE MOTHER looks at THE YOUNG MAN. Long pause
Lights down. Black

IV

Early evening the same day. THE YOUNG MAN is looking out of the window and THE MOTHER is looking at him

THE MOTHER

Don't just stand there
Now you've been standing there
yes it feels as if
you've been standing there
for hours
Either you lie on the bench
or
yes
you stand in front of the window
Short pause
And they're going to come here
too
Yes they're going from house to house
it's strange they haven't been here already
they're going to the others first
yes
short pause
and
breaks off, short pause
No it's so devastating
Short pause
Can't you say something
Pause
You haven't said a single word
for hours
Pause
But you've always been so good and kind
you've never pestered
neither man nor beast
Say something to me
You can't just stay silent

Pause

It's impossible

You're not like that

Long pause

And soon they'll come

soon they'll come here too

Pause

Talk to me

Say something to me

Pause

And you've always been a good boy

Never a lot of get-up-and-go

but good

yes you've always been good

and kind

wouldn't hurt a fly

Pause

Can't you say something to me

Talk to me

Say something

please

THE YOUNG MAN looks at THE MOTHER and grins

But don't stand there and grin

then

Don't do that

Say something

THE YOUNG MAN

What do you want me to say

That it was me who killed him

THE MOTHER

Just say something

say it wasn't you who killed him

THE YOUNG MAN

No

THE MOTHER
    It wasn't you who killed him

THE YOUNG MAN
    That's what I said
    Pause

THE MOTHER
    But
    yes
    but
    but you can't have done it
    Can't you just say that to me
    tell me
    tell me the truth
    say it wasn't you who did it

THE YOUNG MAN
    Yes

THE MOTHER
    You killed him

THE YOUNG MAN
    Yes
    Short pause
    I killed him
    I said
    breaks off

THE MOTHER
    You killed him because he killed your dog

THE YOUNG MAN
    Yes

THE MOTHER
    You killed him

THE YOUNG MAN
    I killed him because he killed my dog

Pause. THE YOUNG MAN goes to the bench and lies down, stares straight ahead.
Long silence

THE MOTHER
You killed him
But
Pause
But then
yes
Pause
And you don't plan to
breaks off. Pause
When they come
what
because they'll come soon
they're going from house to house
And you
pause
you won't
pause
you
pause
you
yes
but say something to me
I'm your mother
say something
talk to me
THE MOTHER walks over to THE YOUNG MAN, shakes his shoulder lightly
I can
breaks off, short pause
Say something to me
We've lived together
you and I
for so many years

we've stayed together
in our way
so say something
won't you
for many years
so don't just lie there
If they take you with them
I'll send you something
get you a guitar
perhaps
a new guitar
a new and good guitar
and say something to me
talk to me
Why can't you
You must say something
don't just lie there like that
You must say something
Pause. There is a knock on the door
I suppose I'll have to open
They're coming now
THE YOUNG MAN sits up on the bench

THE YOUNG MAN

You must open
Pause. There is another knock.
Why don't you open

THE MOTHER

Yes well
Pause. There is another knock

THE YOUNG MAN

I'll have to open
then
*THE YOUNG MAN stands up and walks out and THE MOTHER
walks over to the window, looks out. Pause. THE YOUNG MAN
enters followed by THE FRIEND*

THE FRIEND

Yes we were going to
go out on the fjord
tonight
And the weather's good
And I promised to drop in
but
now
breaks off, quite short pause

THE MOTHER

Yes it's awful
it's unbelievable

THE FRIEND

Yes

THE MOTHER

But it's not
*breaks off, short pause. THE MOTHER leaves and THE YOUNG
MAN walks over to the window*

THE FRIEND

Yes I thought
pause
I thought that I'd
well I promised to drop in
so
Pause
But I don't suppose
it's the day for it
quite short pause
to go out on the fjord
Short pause
Or what
quite short pause
do you say
Pause
I did promise to drop in

so I thought
breaks off
quite short pause

THE YOUNG MAN
We'll have to try again later
some time

THE FRIEND
I suppose

THE YOUNG MAN
Yes
Pause

THE FRIEND
Yes
Pause
But
short pause
well I promised to come and see you
so
that's why
yes

THE YOUNG MAN
We'll have to go out
some other time

THE FRIEND
Yes I just thought
since we'd agreed
breaks off. Pause. THE FRIEND walks over to the window, looks out
What've you buried down there

THE YOUNG MAN
The dog

THE FRIEND
The dog is dead

THE YOUNG MAN
    Yes

THE FRIEND
    I'm sorry
    Pause
    That's why he didn't come back
    Pause

THE YOUNG MAN
    He was lying there dead

THE FRIEND
    I'm really sorry
    Pause
    How sad that he got shot

THE YOUNG MAN
    Who said he got shot

THE FRIEND
    No
    perhaps my mum
    Yes it was her
    she said that the
    that your new neighbour
    had shot your dog

THE YOUNG MAN
    laughs
    One of the last things he did
    right

THE FRIEND
    Yes
    Pause
    No if you
    breaks off, quite short pause

THE YOUNG MAN

We'll have to go out on the fjord and fish
some other time

THE FRIEND

Yes
pause
yes they're going from house to house
asking all sorts of things
they were at our place earlier today
Pause

THE YOUNG MAN

Yes

THE FRIEND

The next time I come home
perhaps
I can drop in
then
okay

THE YOUNG MAN

Yes why don't you
Pause. THE MOTHER enters

THE MOTHER

to THE FRIEND
I should've offered you something
but

THE FRIEND

No
I'm on my way home
To THE YOUNG MAN
Yes I think I'll be going
then
okay
Short pause
We'll have to catch up

next time I get back home

THE MOTHER
Yes thanks for dropping in
And you must drop in again
the next time
you're home

THE FRIEND
Yes I'll do that

THE YOUNG MAN
See you
THE FRIEND leaves. Long pause

THE MOTHER
I suppose we should
breaks off

THE YOUNG MAN
Yes

THE MOTHER
Is there something you want to take with you
THE YOUNG MAN shakes his head
I made you a packed lunch
and
some coffee
yes
and I took
yes
THE MOTHER rushes out and comes back in with a bag
and then I packed some warm clothes for you
And the book you're reading
And the guitar

THE YOUNG MAN
interrupts
I don't have a guitar anymore
Pause

THE MOTHER
If you want to
I can buy you
a new guitar

THE YOUNG MAN
No
Pause

THE MOTHER
Anything else you want to take

THE YOUNG MAN
The dog's collar

THE MOTHER
You want to take the collar
THE YOUNG MAN nods. Pause. There is a knock on the door
We'll be going then

THE YOUNG MAN
Yes

THE MOTHER
questioningly
The collar is hanging in the hall

THE YOUNG MAN
Yes
THE YOUNG MAN leaves and THE MOTHER follows him

Lights down. Black

WWW.OBERONBOOKS.COM

Follow us on www.twitter.com/@oberonbooks
& www.facebook.com/OberonBooksLondon

Printed in the USA
CPSIA information can be obtained
at www.ICGtesting.com
LVHW020955171024
794056LV00004B/1140

9 781783 191284